# VOICES OF COLOR

## ORIGINAL WRITINGS ROOTED IN AUTHENTIC EXPERIENCE

REVISED FIRST EDITION

**Written and edited by Gail A. Bauman, Ph.D.**
Florida A&M University

cognella® | ACADEMIC PUBLISHING

Bassim Hamadeh, CEO and Publisher
Gem Rabanera, Project Editor
Christian Berk, Associate Production Editor
Jess Estrella, Senior Graphic Designer
Trey Soto, Licensing Coordinator
Natalie Piccotti, Director of Marketing
Kassie Graves, Vice President of Editorial
Jamie Giganti, Director of Academic Publishing

Cover image copyright © Depositphotos/rinderart.

Printed in the United States of America

ISBN: 978-1-5165-0891-4 (pbk) / 978-1-5165-0892-1 (br)

**cognella** | ACADEMIC PUBLISHING

# CONTENTS

# PREFACE

In the spring of 2016, as I was packing up my university office in advance of my retirement, I ran across several boxes of writing samples produced by students who had been enrolled in my teacher education classes over the years. These samples had been written over a twenty-five-year span, between 1991 and 2016. As I was packing and sorting, I naturally began to pull out pieces to read and remember. As I did so, I began to recall when some of them had been written. I chuckled at some of their humor. I marveled at the insight of some of the writers' thoughts and felt inspired by some of their words.

So, as I sat there on the floor of my office, surrounded by all these papers, it occurred to me that they were unique and that surely someone besides me should read them. Surely these "voices" should not be packed away somewhere, never to be heard of again.

That was my "aha" moment. That's when I knew I had to find a way for these unique voices to be heard. Fortunately Cognella Academic Publishers agreed that they represented a unique perspective from an often underrepresented group of young people, and that they deserved to be published.

# ACKNOWLEDGMENTS

If it hadn't been for these young people, this book would not have come to be. I would first and foremost like to thank my students, not just the authors of the amazing pieces of writing that made it into this book but all of my students over the course of my career. Thank you for letting me be a part of your lives. Thank you for sharing your innermost thoughts with me. Thank you for trusting me. I hope you learned half as much from me as I learned from you.

I would also like to acknowledge and thank editor extraordinaire Susana Christie, whose kindness, professionalism, and positivity helped to make this book possible. Her suggestions from conception to completion made it a better book. I can say with certainty that *Voices of Color* is truly a collaborative effort made better by Susana's insights and expertise.

Finally, I'd like to thank my best friend (and sometime typist), Kaye Minor, whose love and support over the last thirty years have made me a better teacher and person. I love you honey!

# THE ORIGINS OF VOICES OF COLOR: FROM THE CLASSROOM TO THE REAL WORLD: AN INTRODUCTION

*Voices of Color: Original Writings Rooted in Authentic Experience* is an anthology of powerful personal narratives collected from young adults of color over a twenty-five year period, between 1991 and 2006. This collection of poems, raps, essays, short stories, and so on provides insight into their lives and worlds.

The purpose of this book is to highlight the often underrepresented voices of these young people. Their work gives us insight into their thoughts, their questions, and their ponderings about the world they live in. All of this is expressed in their own words and on their own terms.

When these pieces were written, their authors were juniors and seniors enrolled in a teacher education course at a historically black university in the southeastern United States. In this course, *The Writer's Workshop Approach* (Atwell, 1987) was used. At the heart of this approach are three components of writing: time, ownership, and response. Each writer was given time for real writing and ownership in his or her selection of topic, format, and style. Each writer wrote in his or her own way, receiving feedback and responses from the teacher and fellow students.

This is different from a standard college writing class, in which topics are often assigned, formats prescribed, and length predetermined. This difference is significant, for all of these authors made these decisions for themselves. Their work represents their own original thought, rooted in their own experiences. These writers wrote about what was important to them, what was on their minds. As a result, the topics cover a wide range, with musings on everything from lost loved ones, to the role of the black male in today's society, to reflections on motherhood, sex, and relationships. It is the real stuff of their lives.

The book is called *Voices of Color* to reflect the diversity of the nationalities and ethnicities that these authors brought to the page. The writers include African/Black Americans, Jamaicans, Asians, Nigerians, Puerto Ricans, Iranians, Caucasians, Bahamians, Egyptians, Cubans, and those that are bi- or multiracial, to name just a few.

In order to develop this book, it was necessary to read and analyze several thousand pieces of writing collected over twenty-five years. In doing so, several themes and topics began to emerge, and certain patterns became clear. Some of the themes that emerged from the analysis were predictable such as love. Other topics, however, were a bit more unexpected, like the importance of faith in these authors' lives as well as a variety of relevant political and social topics. Through an analysis of these writings, the primary themes that emerged were identity, respect, justice, love, faith, and hope.

Each chapter is devoted to one of these themes. Although this organizational structure was chosen to group and present the writings, not every piece is about a singular theme. In many instances, themes intertwine and overlap, just as they do in real life. An excellent example is the piece called "Heritage," which, while ostensibly about identity, is also about justice.

Each of the six chapters begins with the theme and its definition, followed by a question or two for readers to think about before they continue. Next, there is an introduction that connects the individual selections to the overall theme. Each individual selection is followed by thought-provoking questions that ask the reader to engage with the writing on a deeper level. At the end of each chapter there are several questions for reflection as well as a choice of prompts that the reader can use to guide journal entries or discussions in reading groups.

These writings are as varied and different as the authors who wrote them. Some of the pieces are meant to challenge readers and provoke thought, while others were written to inspire. Some are meant simply to entertain. Many of the pieces appear to be autobiographical or nonfiction in nature. However, this cannot be assumed, as many are works of imagination and fiction that speak to an author's awareness, if not his or her immediate personal experience. All are worthy of a considered reading, and all are invitations into the views and worlds of these extraordinary young people. Enjoy each of these genuine, thoughtful, passionate *Voices of Color*.

NOTE: All of the authors featured in this anthology were training to be elementary school teachers at the time of the Writer's Workshop. Because elementary school education is still a predominantly female profession, most of the authors are also female. With this in mind, every effort was made to balance male and female perspectives and to include pieces written by men whenever possible.

Finally, the writing samples appear in this book exactly as they were written. In order to maintain the copyright, an editorial decision was made early on to keep the writing genuine— not to change the language or to alter grammar or spelling. We did this also in order to preserve the authentic words and thoughts of the writers. So, to the best of our ability, we have transcribed the pieces faithfully word for word. However, we are only human and any slip up in this respect would have been strictly unintentional.

# CHAPTER 1: IDENTITY

*The culture, beliefs, heritage, language and experiences that make a person (self-identity) or group (group-identity) who they are*

## Who are you? How did you become who you are?

Identity is an especially prevalent theme in the writings of these young people. These authors often wrote to express their identity or to share their personal experiences as young people of color. They reflected on where they came from and paid respect to their heritage and culture. They acknowledged that who they had become, their identity, is an amalgam of their beliefs, heritage, language, and experience.

The first piece, "I Am," traces a woman's heritage from its beginning in Mother Africa to the millennium and Y2K, told from the point of view of each of her ancestors through time. The second selection, "Afro-American Is," reflects on all things Afro-American … "ham hocks, neck bones, cornbread," and so much more.

In "Heritage," the author writes about how her identity was changed by the impact of the events that affected the history of her people forever. She states, we "struggled for change … even when taught to forget." She goes on to write,

"You played God and changed my destiny" and therefore her identity.

In "Blind," a young man questions what it means to be a man in today's world, with the pressures placed on young men, especially young black men by our society. In the piece that follows, "I'm A Man, I Do What Men Do," the author states, "I'm a father, a friend, a brother, a lover. Pull away this mask, there's so much to discover."

A humorous piece, "Phenomenal by Heart, Ghetto by Nature," looks at identity from a different point of view. With wit and warmth, the writer recognizes that sometimes others see us very differently from how we see ourselves. In "Thoughts of a Black Woman," the author states "to the amazement of others, I do think deeply." She defines herself against opposition and predicts that the thoughts of one black woman could change the world.

The last selection, "Grace Avenue," is shocking, painful, and difficult to read as it depicts the impact of a racist childhood incident on the formation of one young girl's identity. After being called by a racist slur for the very first time, the author states, "I tried to make some kind of sense out of my situation, but I couldn't."

# I AM
## Thomasina Brock
### 2008

I AM the Dark Continent, not because of the color of my people's skin, but because so little is known about me.

I AM, Mother Africa.

I AM a weaver; I make a beautiful cloth called Kente and weave it with bright silk thread giving each new design a different name.

I AM the Ashanti tribe.

UM a slave, I's bone on Masa Tunna plantation. Me and muh brotuh Jim, we's be sold to Masa Wilum Tunna in Buk County Jawjah. I's freed thar and ducted in the Nited States Ahmee Hundud-n-thud Cullud Troops under duh command of General Wilum Sherman when he cum thru pilgin n bunnin as he made way to the coast. Neva got muh 40 akas n muh ole moole, but whut I's did git wuz ah legcy for all muh kin to come.

I AM my Great-Grandfather.

I AM a carpenter, though not by trade. You see; I built my house with my own two hands. I had to. I left Jackson County, Florida and journeyed to Apalachicola, Florida to visit my brother Jacob and to work there for a year so that I could save enough money to attend Tuskegee Institute in Tuskegee, Alabama. Upon getting paid, I gave my wages to Jacob for safe keeping, because he was the oldest and thought to be the most responsible. Time soon came for me to leave for school, or so I thought. Jacob had squandered the money. I couldn't afford to return to Jackson County so I made Apalachicola my home.

I AM my Grandfather.

I AM cold here in France but I feel nothing for I am numb. Numb from the sight and stench of death. The war was ruthless and uncaring and the only solace that I found at the time was in the company of a beautiful young woman that I'd met at the USO. It started to rain as we strolled to her house after the dance so I gently draped my coat around her shoulders. The next morning when I returned to retrieve my coat, an elderly stout woman greeted me at the door and told me that the woman that I was looking for was her daughter and that she had been dead for 15 years. She pointed to her gravesite on the side of the house and there I found my coat thrown over the headstone.

I AM my Father.

I AM a fighter, though I don't own a pair of boxing gloves, a weapon, numb chucks, or a knife. You see, I was born with Sickle Cell Anemia so I've had a fight on my hands from the very beginning. In third grade I fought to defend my twin brother from bullies who harassed us daily, during the late sixties and early seventies, I fought with many others in a courageous battle to defend the civil rights of African-Americans. In my early twenties I fought to defend my children and myself from an abusive and alcoholic husband. Heck, I even joined the Army and was part of a senseless battle, and even though I didn't actually fight, my name will forever go down in the annals of history as being there. It seems as if I've been fighting for my life all of my life; but that's o.k. because I know that the battle is not mine but the Lord's.

I AM Me.

I AM strong, proud, intelligent, and beautiful. Some all me a Nubian Princess, though my Father is not a King, nor my Mother from Nubia. Nonetheless, I was blessed as all Princesses are for I developed a passion for cooking and perfected the art, and now no one can resist my Pecan pies or the love that I have for my sons.

I AM my Daughter.

I AM a millennium baby. I was born in Y2K. The world was afraid of and fascinated by this event but I was born unaware and unassuming. For my fifth birthday my Grandmother gave me my first Bible and to show her my gratitude I gave her a kiss that lit a fire in her heart that will never go out. I proved to her that she doesn't have to be perfect to be loved.

I AM my Grandson.

I AM a part of them, and they are a part of me, and so shall it be.

## Questions to Consider

1. In "I AM," the author writes from the point of view of her various ancestors to make a declaration of identity over time. Did you feel that this was an effective technique? Which examples from the piece support your opinion?
2. How many generations were written about in this piece? List them.

# Afro-American Is …

## Kiwana Alexander

1997

Afro-American is collard greens, black-eye peas, sweet potato pie, macaroni and cheese, ham hocks, neckbones, cornbread, and potato salad. Ooh it's so good.

Afro-American is FAMU, Howard, Spelman, Clark-Atlanta, Grambling, Morehouse, Prarie View, Tuskegee, and Southern. A mind is a terrible thing to waste.

Afro-American is you go girl, whatever, true, what's up, I ain't mad at ya, and you so crazy. Ebonically speaking is this standard english?

Afro-American is bobs, braids, ball-heads, weaves, naturals, afros, curley perms, dreds, and texturizers. What in the world happened to yo head?

Afro-American is the Bank Head Bounce, the Wop, the Moon Walk, Forrest Gump, California Worm, the Butterfly, the Squirrel, and Reebok. Can we stop doing the same dances to every song we hear?

Afro-American is Marcus Garvey, Malcom X, Martin Luther King, Rosa Parks, Sojourner Truth, Harriet Tubman, Medgar Evers, and C.K. Steel. They held us down but couldn't keep us back.

Afro-American is Maya Angelou, Alice Walker, Oprah Winfrey, Terry McMillan, Angela Bassett, and My Mother (Michelle Nelson). The epitome of beautiful black women.

Afro-American is loving one another, respecting each other, showing our inner pride, and realizing one must survive.

Afro-American is power!

## Questions to Consider

1.  The term *Afro-American* is no longer commonly used. During what decade was this terminology popular?
2.  What terms do we use now to describe this ethnic group?
3.  What other terminology has been used in the past?

# Heritage

## Glennette Richardson

2002


We came too late.
Experienced but in time,
Enough to make an imprint,
A memory.

They say, "Wait!
You can't eat here,
Coloreds served in the back!"
"You can't live here, whites only."

And, I am supposed to forgive,
While I stand here on the edge of hell,
Starved half dead for change!

While they tell us,
*"Nigger, you standing here face to face*
*Looking on to a great white race."*


Do you not understand?
Why you've got that dirty color
On your face?

What rights?
Whose rights?
Do you want to be free?
Or do you want to live?

Struggle, Strive
Back down only to imprint a path.

I have only
Hours to make count.
To avoid is to go nowhere.

To embrace is to change.
To know is only half the battle

To experience and venture is to seize the day,
Veni, Vidi, Vici,
I came, I saw, I conquered.

Struggles for change,
Experienced to remember,
Even when taught to forget.

How dare you tell me to leave!
Did you not bring my battered soul here?

You say get off my land,
I assume, my sir,
That you are Native American.
You played God and changed my destiny,
So, when I say this is my heritage,
This is all I know
And will never forget.

## Questions to Consider

1. In "Heritage" the author talks about how her destiny and therefore her identity were changed forever by the events affecting her people. How is this theme relevant today?
2. How are people's lives being affected by today's social policies?

# Blind

## Abyon McInnis

2013

We are blind, blinded by society's expectations of how things should be. If you don't believe me, please answer this question: What does it mean to be a man? A good man.

When these types of questions arise, many people have these "Mr. Perfect" images in mind. That is not realistic. Who has the right to say that someone is not a good man? Is it because 'society' says he doesn't make enough money, have a fancy car, or a decent education? Society'... Yea, that's a credible source.

Society is BLIND! We are blinded by the media, blinded by our peers, and blinded by stereotypes that surround us on a daily basis. When celebrities show money, flashy jewelry, and nice clothes this is what we see as the 'good life'. Why is it that this is what we associate with being a man? Being a man is not something that can be stripped away from an individual because he does not meet someone else's expectations.

Being a good man has many unwritten rules such as paying for dates, opening doors, and being Mr. Perfect. God himself does not judge a man until the end of his days. Why should you and I? Please, let's open our eyes so that we can realize being a man comes from within. It is not decided by our peers, the media, or society. Why should they be the judge of who is or isn't a good man? Being a man is not an option! However, a man must choose the type of man he wants to be.

## Questions to Consider

1. In "Blind" the author contends that a man must choose the type of man he wants to be. Do you believe that a man, particularly a black man, can freely make that choice for himself in today's society? Why or why not?

2. Do you feel that these same expectations apply to other men of color? Why or why not?

# I'm A Man, I Do What Men Do

## George E. Bruton III

**2005**

I'm a man, I do what men do.
This is not to praise or inspire, or to educate you.

Just a little something something, I'm getting off my chest.
It might even amuse you, I'm giving it my best.

From caveman to method man, some things just never change.
Always looking for the moment, your thoughts I'll rearrange.

I look, I love, I want, I need.
That's what it takes to plant my seed.

I'm a sucker for the eyes, nice curves, and soft thighs.
And a foreign accent gives me such a rise.

Caring for my family with money and protection.
It's tough sometimes seeming impossible, but God gives me direction.

I'm a father, a friend, a brother, and a lover.
Pull away this student mask, there's so much to discover.

Trying to keep it real, I like to impress.
I try not to lie, I'm not perfect, I confess.

I'm a spiritual brother, an artist and very "deep".

Getting up there in age, my youth I'd love to keep.
I too have many issues, I think that we all do

Without them the world would be boring, so I'll try to work on thru.
Didn't make up none of the rules for these love and sex games we play.
I'll take it one day at a time, I think I'll be okay.

I should not say that I'm a man, just see it in my actions.
All these things I think are common, I can get satisfaction.

## Questions to Consider

1. Do you know anyone like the man in "I'm a Man, I Do What Men Do?" Is this an accurate portrayal?
2. If you were to describe what a man does, what would be included in your description? Would it be similar to or different from this author's ideas?

# Phenomenal by Heart, Ghetto by Nature

## Diamond Paramore

2015


Am I too ghetto?
No, I'm not too ghetto.
Just because I walk to the corner store,
Poppin' my lips and shakin' my hips.

I know I'm not too ghetto.
Because I shop at Walmart,
Wearing my stilettos and pushing my cart.
Not ashamed to say,
I love me some Pop Tarts.

I know I'm not too ghetto
Just because I got rollers in my hair,
And yea, some stop and some stare,
Because I'm fine and very rare.

I know I'm not too ghetto,
Just because I'm not "boojie",
And prefer to wear Coojie,
Than Marc Jacob or Fendi.
I can still be trendy.

I know I'm not too ghetto,
Because I receive food stamps,
And on occasion have been called a tramp.
I got six baby daddies and no man.
As a single mother,
I do the best that I can.

I know I'm not too ghetto,
Because I work at strip clubs.
To make extra money,
I offer private rubs.

I know I'm not too ghetto,
Because I get money fast.
Academically I always pass.
So any man lucky enough to have me,
Will tell you I'm not their first, but their last,
Because I have loads of class and far too much sass.

I know I'm not too ghetto,
Because I am articulate and sexy inside and out.
You can tell by listening to me what I'm all about.

So, no I'm not too ghetto!
I sign my own checks and make my own deals.
I'm a five star bitch eating five star meals.
My name is Diamond and I am a queen,
So when you say I'm too ghetto,
What the hell do you mean?

## Questions to Consider

1. How does the woman in "Phenomenal by Heart, Ghetto by Nature" feel about herself? How do you know this?
2. How do you think other people really see her? Make a T chart and compare her perception of herself to other people's perceptions of her.

# Thoughts of a Black Woman

## Kimberley E. Brown
2004

To the amazement of others,
I do think deeply.
And not of black bodies moving in the dark,
But of black minds looking for solutions.
Of black children reaching for the stars.
Of black mothers nurturing their young,
And of trees and flowers and love.

I think of the blackness of my skin
And the offense it sometimes brings to others.
No matter how much I wash it,
There is no difference.

So, I make the decision to hold my head up real high.
It is then that I realize,
I am what I am.
No mortal man or woman,
Can make me something I am not.

And I realize that the love of this black woman
Can affect this world
And the thoughts of this black woman
Just might change the world.

## Questions to Consider

1. Do you believe, as the author of "Thoughts of a Black Woman" does, that the thoughts of one person can change the world?
2. Can you think of one person whose thoughts have done just that? What example or examples would you give to support your opinion?
3. How does the author feel about herself? How would you describe her identity?

# Grace Avenue

## Kati Mobley

**1994**

"Nigger"!

The word felt like a bullet bursting through my chest.

"Go home, nigger!"

I heard it again. I ran as fast as I could fearing for what might happen if they caught me, and knowing that I could not out run them.

"Why"!

I kept repeating in my head, as I ran to make it to Grace Avenue.

"Leave us alone!"

I heard my cousin shout as she pulled me to go faster. She ran faster than I did, and she knew they would catch me if I didn't speed up. I could feel my chest contracting, I couldn't seem to get enough air. I didn't look back, hoping that if I couldn't see them they would disappear.

"Oh My God"!

They had me!

"We hate niggers!"

One of them said as he pushed me down. I saw Edie coming to help out of the corner of my eye, but one of them grabbed her and threw her to the ground as well.

"We hate nigger lovers too!"

They shouted at my cousin in voices that sounded like the devil himself. I could feel the hard cement against my arm, and I felt the grass and leaves in my face. I couldn't get up, someone was stepping on my back. They forced their rage mainly on me, and my cousin was able to get up and get away.

"I'm Telling"!

She shouted, as she ran towards Grace Avenue crying. I guess this scared them a little bit because I felt the foot leave my back. By now tears were streaming down my face, but I took advantage of the moment and got up to run. They caught me before I was all the way up and took turns spitting in my face while holding my hands behind my back. I couldn't move. I couldn't wipe it away. I couldn't do anything.

"Why"! "Why"!

Suddenly I heard a voice in the distance. A car was passing by and I guess the driver saw my distress.
"Hey, What are you doing!"
His comment scared them, but he did not stop to aid me. They let me go and took off running the other way. I started running as fast as I could also, hoping I could make it the rest of the way. With tears streaming down my face I ran and ran until I saw the sign, Grace Avenue. I felt safe on my street, and I was too out of breath to continue running anymore. I tried to

make some kind of sense out of my situation, but I couldn't. I had anticipated this day for a long time, and now for it to end this way I couldn't comprehend a reason why.

"What is a nigger?"

"Why do they hate me?"

"What did I do wrong?"

"Does this happen to everyone their first day of kindergarten?"

These all seemed like good questions, but I couldn't answer them. It was a very long time before I understood that there is no answer that could justify what they had done to me.

## Questions to Consider

1. Describe the impact of the incident described in "Grace Avenue" on the author's identity.
2. How did this piece make you feel?
3. Have you ever experienced anything similar to this?

## Reflections

1. Which one of the pieces in this section did you like the most/least? Why?
2. To which of the pieces in this section could you most/least relate? How? Why?

3. The overall theme of this section is identity. How did each piece in this section reflect that theme?
4. What do you think contributes to a person's identity? Do you think our identities are generated internally, externally, or both? Explain your answer.
5. How can one person, or a people, overcome the identity ascribed to them by others?
6. How are current policies on immigration impacting the identity of different ethnic groups within our society today?

## Journal Prompts

1. Select one family member, living or deceased. Now try to hear his or her voice in your head. Write a paragraph or two in that voice from your family member's perspective. Include expressions, words, phrases, and so on that they use or used often.
2. How would you describe your own identity? Who are you? Write an introductory statement about yourself for someone you have never met.
3. What makes you who you are? Where did your identity from come? Write about what you believe have been the biggest influences to shape your identity.
4. Interview some family members and draw a family tree to the best of your ability with the information you have. Write a reflection statement about what you have learned.

# CHAPTER 2: RESPECT

*To hold in regard, to honor, to esteem or to think of highly*

## How important is it to you to feel respected in your life? How important is self-respect?

As you read the pieces in this chapter, you will see that respect and self-respect are very important to these authors. The chapter opens with "Respect Her Wishes," in which a young man speaks to other young men about what they should do when a girl says no.

In "Can You Hear Me," a young woman shares her desire not only to be seen by men but also to be heard and valued. "Can you hear me earning my degree, grasping all the knowledge offered to me?" While in "The Likes of Me," a different young woman wonders if wearing a short skirt and strutting around with sass would get a boy to notice her. Ultimately she decides that if this is what she has to do to get attention from a boy, he doesn't deserve her. Self-respect wins out.

In a completely different take on self-respect, "These Last Ten Dollars" features a young woman who has fallen on hard times. She writes with humor about the money left in her pocket and what she's going to do about that.

"Daddy, Is This an Appropriate Name for You?" introduces the reader to a young woman struggling with her feelings about her respect/lack of respect for father and the impact of those feelings. While in "I Don't Know" the writer asks herself a series of increasingly serious questions about her whereabouts and what has just happened to her.

In the essay titled "Michelle Obama," the author speaks of a different kind of respect ... respect as inspiration and aspiration. She expresses her admiration and respect for the first black first lady.

The final piece in this chapter is titled "Only a Black Mother." It discusses the things only a black mother would do, like "only a black mother beats you for something your brother or sister did, just because you were around ... and only a black mother offers to call the child abuse hotline for you!"

As you will see as you read, each piece in this section deals with respect and/or self-respect. These authors wrote about the people and things they held in high regard and to honor the concepts and ideas of which they thought highly.

# Respect Her Wishes

## Joseph Robinson

**1995**

When a girl says no,
Don't get mad.
Don't think of the fun,
That you could have had.
When a girl says no,
Leave her alone.
If you can't take it,
Then take her back home.

When a girl says no,
She is a lady.
She made her choice,
She's not a cry baby.

When a girl says no,
It is her right.
Don't go raisin' hell,
Or startin' a fight.


When a girl says no,
Don't get suspicious.
Just take a cold shower,
And respect her wishes.

## Questions to Consider

1. Do you think the author of "Respect Her Wishes" is giving good advice to other young men? What other advice might he have given?
2. Does this young man's perspective surprise you in any way?

# Can You Hear Me?

Erin M. Forde

**2005**

Can you hear me?
Walking down the street, so fine and so proud
Letting the onlookers know,
A real woman is walking by and not the average street hoe.

Can you hear me?
Demanding respect
Making sure that people understand that I earn everything I get.
From the clothes on my back to the shoes on my feet.
I pay for all these things
Even the glasses that you see.

Can you hear me?
Earning my degree
Grasping all available knowledge offered to me.
Ensuring that I become an educated Black woman
not a possible parolee.

Can you hear me?
Fighting for our love to shine through.
Letting you know off top that those "Baby baby pleases" will not do.
If you want to be with me, you have to commit
I am the wrong chick to try some slickness with.

So I ask you
Before I give my mind, body, and heart to you.
Before I commit myself to a lifetime of loving you
I need to know first….
Can you hear me?

## Questions to Consider

1.  Why is this piece called "Can You Hear Me?" rather than "Can You See Me?" What is the difference in hearing or seeing someone?
2.  Who do you think is the intended audience for this piece?
3.  How does the author's question tie in to the idea of respect?

# The Likes of Me

Endia Walton

**2010**

Maybe if I wore a short, short, skirt or strutted the halls with sass,
Or maybe if I acted like the cool girls, & skipped a couple of my classes.
Naw, my mom would kill me, so I'll think of another route;
Maybe I'll participate in the school talent show so he can hear my name being shouted?
But what if he doesn't go & I sang that song for nothing.
Maybe I'll try out for the basketball water girl, so I'll have an excuse for handing him something.

Maybe I'll just put weave in or change my hair so I won't go unnoticed,
Jazz my toes and fancy my nails, then I'll steal his focus.
I shouldn't stop there; I'll add some tattoos and put my body on display,
Then I'll be like a piece of artwork waiting for someone to pay.
What am I thinking I wouldn't do those things just for someone to see,
Because God says if they didn't notice by now,
Then they don't deserve the likes of me.

## Questions to Consider

1. In "The Likes of Me" the author has written in the first person, using the voice of a child. Why do you think she chose to do this?
2. How would the piece be different if it had been written in another voice?
3. How old is the narrator of this piece? What evidence can you cite to support this conclusion?

# Daddy, Is This an Appropriate Name for You?

## Darlene Fagin

2000

Were you there to hold my hand-
To block my fall-to say yes you can?
All these years I wondered in my head-
Where's my daddy, is he dead?

Years went by without a clue,
Everyone wondered where were you.
You stayed over for a little while, but once
Again you disappeared without a trace-
And took my smile.

By this time I'm all grown up.
you came back-I was surprised
And this was the year my respect died.

You lied, you stole, you cheated, mistreated-
My sister, my brother, and especially my mother.
You tried to take her away from me,
But it was not her time to leave.

I finished high school
And now I'm in college,
Making something of myself.

All these years you have missed-
You could have been a part of this.

## Questions to Consider

1.  What emotions underlie "Daddy: Is This an Appropriate Name for You?"
2.  Does the author respect her father? What are the clues to how she feels?

# These Last Ten Dollars

## Karrie Cockrum

2006

These last ten dollars in my pocket got me hurtin'.
Should I be a player, take these fools money, quick to flirtin'.
Or should I be that good girl-stuck in my ways.
Or should I be that bad girl-line em' up and get paid.

Hell, it's the end of days or at least the end of the week.
A sister want to live and a sister got to eat.
I hunger for love like I hunger for food, but what could really come of a
sister out here trying to play these dudes?

So I sit down like 50 and come up with 21 questions.
Like, should I approach these fools, start cheesin' or blushin'?
Should I turn my head and pretend to be rushin'?
Let my feet stomp hard-till you can hear the percussion.

Well, it's just a situation.
I either win or I lose.
Have a little self-respect?
Or let him buy me some new shoes?

## Questions to Consider

1. How would you describe the moral dilemma faced by the author in "These Last Ten Dollars"?
2. How does the author use humor to deflect from the seriousness of her situation?
3. Do you think she respects herself? Do you respect her?

# I Don't Know
## Te'Andria Moore
2013

Where am I?
How long have I been here?
Where are my clothes?
I don't know.

Where are my keys?
Where are my friends?
Where is my car?
I don't know.

What am I to do?
Who must I call?
Who will listen?
Who will believe me?
I don't know.

Who can I trust?
Why did this happen to me?
I don't know.

Should I shower?
Should I stay?
What's my next move?
I don't know.

Will he do it again?
How come I can't remember?
Did it hurt?
Oh my gosh!
Is that blood?
I don't know.

My clothes are gone.
My skin is bruised.
My heart is broken.
Deep down inside.
I do know.

## Questions to Consider

1. Do you find the questioning technique used in "I Don't Know" to be effective?
2. How do you think this piece relates to respect and self-respect?
3. At what point in this piece did you figure out what had happened to the narrator?

# Michelle Obama

## Inika Pierre

**2008**

Many people have questioned me about my profound interest and admiration for Michelle Obama during and after the campaign. Don't get me wrong, I am in great support of our president Barack Obama. However, when Michelle confidently graced the spotlight during the Democratic National Convention, engaged in fruitful conversation on "The View" and exuded confidence and eloquence in important interviews with Larry King, she became the caliber of role model I would like to fulfil. Towards the end of the election, I was confident in Michelle Obama as America's sweetheart and new First Lady.

In the many days since the election, Michelle has been showcased in various magazines—*Newsweek*, *Essence* and *Time*, just to name a few. With every article, Michelle has mirrored the faces of black women in America today. She is a fresh new iconic figure in American culture, who can identify with the day-to-day problems of her supporters.

I support this woman who never overreaches her husband, but serves as his confidant and equal partner. I applaud this woman whose origins come from humble beginnings in Chicago to excel at the country's top institutions. I commend this woman who embraces motherhood and juggles it along with a demanding career.

Michelle Obama radiates the confidence that my mother gives when she walks into a room, the family values my grandmother has instilled in her kin, the femininity and lady-like qualities of my aunts, and the determination and drive of my sisters. Michelle is phenomenal. When I envision Michelle Obama, I envision me.

## Questions to Consider

1. How does the author of this piece feel about Michelle Obama? Why does she feel this way?
2. Have you ever admired or respected someone in the way the author of this essay respects and admires Michelle Obama? Who was it? Why did you feel that way?

# Only a Black Mother

Traci R. Cohen

2006

Only a black mother calls you out of your room, from upstairs to downstairs, to find the remote, change the channel, or fix her a glass of ice water.

Only a black mother hits you with anything in reach
(a shoe, an extension cord, or a cup).

Only a black mother makes you pick out your own switch off
 of the tree, and if it is too small she makes you go back
to pick a bigger one.

Only a black mother hits you in the head with a brush
while getting your hair done, because you are too
 busy concentrating on your favorite television show.

Only a black mother burns you with a straightening comb
and yells, "Hold your head up!"

Only a black mother threatens to beat you in front of the class
when you bring a horrible report card home.
Only a black mother beats the life out of you and then asks,
"What are you crying for?"

Only a black mother pronounces every syllable while beating
 you with the biggest belt in the house.
"Didn't-I-tell-you-not-to-do-that-any-more?"

Only a black mother beats you for something your brother or sister did, just because you were around.

Only a black mother offers to call the child abuse hotline for you.

Only a black mother picks up the phone when you've snuck on it in the middle of the night and embarrasses you.

Only a black mother can slap the taste out of your mouth.

Only a black mother can be appreciated and loved for these things in the long run.

## Questions to Consider

1. Were you surprised by the ending of "Only a Black Mother"? What were you expecting?
2. How does the author feel about her mother overall? Does she respect her mother?
3. What is the importance of this particular poem and its depiction of a mother's role?

# Reflections

1. All of the pieces included in this section are related to the theme of respect, including self-respect. To which piece or pieces do you most and least relate and why?
2. What was your favorite selection? Your least favorite? Why?
3. Which piece do you think had the strongest voice? Give examples to support your answer.
4. Which of the writings most represents a traditional notion of respect?
5. Which piece surprised you the most?

# Journal Prompts

1. Who do you most respect in this world? Why do you respect this person? Write a short biographical sketch of him or her, explaining the reasons for your feelings and what he or she means to you.
2. Tell about a time when you were disrespected. Write about the incident and describe how it made you feel.
3. Take a long look at yourself in the mirror. Do you respect what you see? Do you respect some parts of yourself but not all? Write a paragraph that describes what you see. Write a second paragraph that describes what you respect or don't respect about the person in the mirror.
4. Brainstorm a list of the different forms that respect takes in these pieces. Add some of your own ideas about the different forms of respect. Choose one and write a paragraph describing this kind of respect.

# CHAPTER 3: JUSTICE

*Fairness, equity, just behavior or treatment*

## In today's world, do you think that everyone, regardless of race, religion, sexual orientation, gender, etc., is treated justly? Can justice ever be truly blind?

The readings in this chapter explore the experiences, equities, and inequities in the world as seen from these authors' perspectives as young people of color. The selections address timely, relevant, and important issues including discrimination, violence, access to equal opportunities, and civil liberties.

The first piece, "The Death of a Son," is a powerful, poignant depiction of a mother's loss of her child to indiscriminate and senseless gun violence. In "Yes, I'm Black," the author discusses the injustices perpetrated on one another by light- and dark-skinned blacks.

"Growing Up" deals with real and perceived justice/injustice for women. The next piece, "Money Changes Everything," examines what happens to people when they get some money and how their actions are perceived as just or unjust by their families, friends, and community.

The "Depths of My Pain" deals with social justice. In it the author challenges the injustices of "the system." He says that "Something must be done so I don't become a victim, But ain't nothin' gonna change unless you change the system."

Next, "The Bus Ride Home" compares and contrasts the struggles and perspectives of two young mothers. "Cry" offers the reader a view of the "thug life" and what it means to live it, hustling every day to support a family, habits, and more.

The final essay in this section is a plea for young people today to "Wake Up." "While I'm slumped over on my ragged knees looking for a means to escape, you young folk hang around on Saturday night hoping you'll be called for a date."

Each piece, in its own way, explores the concept of justice, equity, or fairness in the worlds of these authors, which may reinforce their own views or stand as a heartfelt reminder that in today's world, true justice still eludes us.

# The Death of a Son

Latrina Taylor

**2004**


Sitting in a dimmed room
Filled with people shedding tears,
Grieving abundantly,
And expressing their worst fears.

"Oh my God",
"No! No!"
"How?" and "Why?"
Are the questions that exist deep down inside.

He was only eighteen,
About to graduate from high school,
He was recently accepted into college,
But now his life is through.

Just a week ago he was full of laughter and cheer,
Excited about what life had to offer,
And it was certainly clear.

This all ended instantly,
With three bullets to the chest
A victim of street violence,
That resulted in his death.

He leaves to cherish
His family and friends,
Who vow to honor him,
For as long as they live.

"But today is a sad one"
Is what his mother screams,
Because she is burying her son,
And is left with only his memory.

## Questions to Consider

1. Have you ever experienced an incident of street violence? Do you know anyone who has? Even if you have no personal experience, what do you think the impact of this kind of experience is?
2. If this is something you only hear about on the news, what assumptions do you catch yourself making about those involved? Does "Death of a Son" make you question those assumptions? How?

# Yes, I'm Black

## Chris Osborne

2005


I know my skin complexion may be light
But that's only because my relative was raped by somebody white

My hair may be curly, my gums might be pink
But I beg you please don't for one second think

That the amount of melanin my skin may possess
Makes me any different, better, more, or less

I'm still a minority living in a majority's world
The racism I face is just as hateful and cold

I get followed around in stores like I'm playing African-American tag
When the clerks should really be watching the two blonde girls
filling up their Dooney & Bourke bags

I get pulled over for doing five over the limit
And even though I get a warning instead of a ticket


It hurts to know I was stopped just because of the color of my skin
But then I have to ask myself what kind of world am I in

When my so-called brothers and sisters question my race
This shows me why our culture is viewed with so much disgrace

There's no light skin or dark skin, good hair or bad hair
Just look around you, there's nothing but black students in here

So no matter how much color my skin may lack
No I'm not mixed or Hispanic, but...
YES I'M BLACK!

## Questions to Consider

1. Do you think that what the author is saying is true?
2. Is there racism and/or discrimination between/ among light- and dark-skinned blacks? If so, provide some real life examples.
3. To your knowledge, is there racism and/or discrimination in other cultures based on skin color?

# Growing Up
## Dawn-Geri Grissett
2004

Once upon a time I was a girl.
I was a girl, small and meek, lost in this big world.
This big world that wouldn't seem so big one day.
One day as I grew, the world grew too.
The world grew too and I was still small and meek.
Small and meek as a woman, still growing.
Still growing in a world that's growing with me.
Growing with me but, at the same time, not letting me grow.
Not letting me grow because men still hold the highest positions.
The highest positions as presidents and kings.
Presidents and kings with strong women standing by their sides.
Standing by their sides because we aren't seen as strong enough.
Strong enough to take over a country or be president.
Be a president of a country in this big world.
In this big world where women seem so small and meek.
Small and meek in a world that won't let us grow.

## Questions to Consider

1. Do you feel, as the author does, that women are seen as small and meek and can never be elected to the highest positions?
2. In light of what has recently happened politically in the United States, do you believe a woman can be a world leader or a president? Why or why not?

# Money Changes Everything

## Markia Cunningham

**2005**


I once knew this guy,
That was down to earth,
But that all changed, once he claimed his so-called rebirth.
He started out hanging with the thugs in the hoods,
Being on the corner til' five in the morning, trying to slang wood.
When he made the dramatic change of turning for good,
None of his former "boys" quite understood.
Back when he was doing wrong,
He was still so very cool,
He would always encourage the young kids in the neighborhood to go
to school.
When the opportunity came for him to become a super star,
He immediately took the chance and went away far.
Now he's earning millions of dollars,
And won't even stop by to give his old friends a "holla!"
His mother needed a couple of dollars to pay her electric bill,
So, she decided to ask her son in hopes that he will.
He didn't beat around the bush with her at all,
Instead, he straight up told her "NO" and disconnected her call.
When his old community needed him financially to support a couple
of teens, who
Wanted to go to college,
His reply was, "Who needs knowledge?"
He then went on to say, "I made it big without it, so can they and I wish
people would stop

Looking at me as their personal way of pay."
Although he continued with his glamorous life,
His family still didn't wish him any strife.
He never gave back to the community, from which he came,
And in the end, he gained even more fame!
People always say money is the root of all evil.
I am really starting to believe it is true,
Because once a "nigga" get a dollar, he begins to act brand new.
As you can see,
Money changes everything!

## Questions to Consider

1. In this piece a young man comes into some money and everyone begins to look at him as "their personal way of pay." When people begin to ask him for money, he turns them down. Is he justified in saying no to them? Why or why not?
2. What, if any, obligation did this man have to "pay" support to his family, friends, and community?
3. What, if any, obligation do any of us have to give back to family, friends, and/or community in return for their support?

# Depths of My Pain
## Christopher Johnson
**2006/2016**


A moment of clarity because I need to clear my thoughts,
About the lies that were sold and the dreams that were bought.

Freedom ain't free, never has and never will be.
I've learned that you will never have freedom if you look like me.

They try to fool you with diversity and this illusion of inclusion,
Just to find out that the illusion of inclusion is actually exclusion.

They tell you to be mindful, be humble and stay woke,
But how can I fix a system that they don't know is broke.

The system doesn't work for people who look like you and me,
Just a few tokens here and there to make you think that we are free.

I've heard that you have to be twice is good just to get half as far,
But you really have to be a hundred times better to get to where they are.

Something must be done so I don't become a victim,
But ain't nothin' gonna change unless you change the system.
So do all you can and help others as much as you help yourself,
Though many times I try to give food for thought, but they'd rather
starve themselves.

## Questions to Consider

1. In "Depths of My Pain," how does the author feel about 'the system'? Why does he feel this way?
2. What does the author mean when he says, "they try to fool you with diversity and this illusion of inclusion"?

# The Bus Ride Home

## Roshan Hamilton

2000

Nobody likes to ride the bus and I was mad because I had to take one home yesterday. But, I took a bus ride and I saw real life as I watched the contrast between two mothers.

One mother held her baby as he played peek-a-boo with an elderly woman. Simplicity and happiness beaming from the child's eyes, making me happy and putting a smile on my face.

As I turn, I see another young mother with the weight of the world on her shoulders. I try to smile at her two little girls, while my heart is breaking inside. They look at me as if they do not know what a smile is. There is a look of awe on their faces like they want to experience the sensation of a smile. All the while their mother is running her short life through her mind, wondering how this happened. This thing called life and why it has turned out this way. So many emotions running deep in her eyes crying out from her soul, not wanting her children to experience the pain and reality of real life, yet knowing that it is inevitable.

One mother holding her baby and comforting him. The other not daring to show affection. She thinks she is doing the right thing. All the while my heart is hurting because this scenario is all too familiar to me.

In my heart I call out to God to take their pain away.

Oh, yeah, remember, the thought I had before getting on the bus? The one where I was mad about having to take the bus?

It is gone.

## Questions to Consider

1. "The Bus Ride Home" presents the reader with images of two young mothers on a bus with their children. Draw a diagram and compare and contrast the thoughts and behaviors of these mothers.
2. Which mother do you think has a better chance of setting her children up for success in the future? Why?

# Cry

## Lord J. Ryder

2001

Parlaying deep within the urban allure
Unsure of exactly what god's gracious gift of life has in store
Shadows of a man seen stalking the avenues
Drinking in the blues
Of another wave of homies making their screen debuts
On the eleven o'clock news
Poster boy of a generation of violence
That only underscores the horrors caused by a community silenced
Family and loved ones lost to guns at the hands of sons
Dying for a life better than the one we were prescribed......
This is what it sounds like when thugs cry

Photos of inmates placed on dresser shelves
Playful poses of population's primary proprietors peeking at hell
Ritualized sacrifices to a government with no god
And we get sucked deep under, under the guise of being hard
Late night screams of the niggas you looked up to getting raped
Early morning scenes of strip searches and the same iron gates
You see, you can kind of forget in your dreams in what condition you reside
But when you awake, this is what it sounds like when thugs cry
Oh, the joy of bringing a new life into the slums
Confusing position of being a father to a son
And I never had one
Seeking a better life in the only form I know how?
Not allowed,
My baby's mama wants a daddy that can have her son proud

But she's used to the money my hustle provides
And a legit gig is an inevitable breakdown in disguise
And I'm tired, browbeaten from belittling white boys showing me how to make fries
Remembering when the only quarter pound with cheese I knew, was stacks and baking pies

The pay cut? Sheesh, divide earlier times by ten to the nine
Minus social security and Income taxing mine
Stomachaches from lack of papes are killing my pride
Contemplating suicide to escape this troubled time
In less than a week I switched back to the drug sales that fed my seed
Baby mom's greed lets her receive the monetary support that I feed

Then the cops stop me for all the coke and weed
The judge ordered life cause that was strike three
And the two people I gave my life for?
never stop by
…………This is what it sounds like when thugs cry.

## Questions to Consider

1. What is the overall meaning and message of "Cry"?
2. What, if anything, do you think the author has learned from his experiences?

# Wake Up
## Anastasia E. Means
**1997**

Wake up my children, didn't you hear what I said?
I know that you're still sleeping instead of trying to get ahead.

While I'm slumped over on my rugged knees looking for a means to escape,
You young folk hang around on Saturday night hoping you'll be called for a date.

Get up! Can't you hear? You've got it much better than me,
I had to plan an Underground Railroad to set my people free.

I really don't understand the young folk of today,
After all my years of sweat and tears, all you can do is lay.

Always making excuses of why you're not a success,
One day my child you'll realize that you were reared from the best.

There wouldn't be an America without the power of our voice,
So wake up my children, it's time you made that choice.

Don't get me wrong, I don't mean to fuss,
I've realized that we have moved to the front of the bus.

But whether we remain there depends on you,
One day you'll soon realize what I'm saying is true.

The struggle continues even today,
Don't get too comfortable, we still have a long way.

I can't believe that you won't even go out and vote,
I hope you realize these issues affect black folk.

Don't let my sweat and tears be in vain,
God gave you a blessing when he created the brain.

## Questions to Consider

1. Who is speaking in this piece? Whose voice do you hear? How do you know? Give examples from the poem.
2. At what point in the poem did you figure out who was speaking?
3. What is the speaker trying to tell the young people of today? What is her message?

# Reflections

1. The overall theme of this section is justice. How does each piece in this section reflect that theme?
2. After reading these selections, what do these authors seem to believe about justice? Do you think they believe that everyone—regardless of race, religion, sexual orientation, and so on—is treated fairly and justly in today's world? Choose at least one piece to illustrate your point.

# Journal Prompts

1. Have you ever been in a situation where you felt unfairly or unjustly treated? Write about that incident and how it made you feel.
2. Find a current events article about an issue related to justice (and/or injustice) that supports or relates to one of the pieces in this section. Write a paper explaining how the article supports or refutes the premise of the writer.
3. Do you believe that justice is blind? Write a short piece including at least three facts supporting your belief that justice is or is not blind.

# CHAPTER 4: LOVE

*Affection, benevolence, goodwill, or deep concern for the welfare of another*

## What is love? How many different kinds of love are there?

Since the authors of the selections in this chapter were primarily university students between the ages of eighteen and twenty-five, the topic of love and relationships was often on their minds. They wrote poems about romance, falling in and out of love, finding the right person, and other relationship issues. They wrote about the things that they love and the people they love, whether family, friends, or intimate partners.

The first piece, "Tango," explores the dance of love and the ways in which a relationship is often like a tango. "You leap, I follow ... hand in hand you lead this dance." "White/ Black" addresses the complexities of a changing love, a love for white that, with time, gives way to an acceptance of and love for black.

In "How to Love a Black Man" the writer tries to help the reader understand why it isn't easy to love a black man, while "Mister Misunderstood" features a very different perspective. This second piece speaks of the writer's long-distance love for her man, a man who has never truly been understood by the world and society in which they both live. In her poem, she states that she is "holdin' it down 'til the day they set you free!"

The next piece, "A Man's Voice," is included to balance out the female voices on love in this chapter. In this piece, the author says, "Believe or not, some of us will cook you dinner and run your bath water. On you, some of us will spend our last quarter."

Love between fathers and daughters is the focus of "You Are the First Man I Ever Loved" and "Thank You," although these two works tell of very different relationships. Finally, "My First Love" surprises the reader with its description of an ardent young man dealing with a new and very special relationship.

As you can see, the topic of love in its many forms was often a subject of real importance to these young writers. As they lived it, so they wrote about it. They reveled in love, grappled with love, and ultimately found forgiveness through love.

# Tango

## Kayla Marchel

2014

Me and you, hand in hand
Step by step, you lead this dance.

From the start, our hearts are one.
Not letting go until this dance is done.

In the beginning things are smooth.
The rhythm is right, we're in a groove.

You lead, I follow, no questions asked.
Your heart lead us, you swear we'll last.

The music picks up, you lose your place.
I try to keep up, but our dance is now a race.

You go one way, I go another.
Our hearts disconnect, we lose one another.

You want to dip, I want to leap.
How did things get so out of control? We were so deep.
You are flustered and all over the place
So, I try to step in and take the lead with grace.

But sadly our hearts beat out of sync.
We've lost the steps quick as a wink.

Who would have thought that a year ago,
Our love would be nothing but a tango.

## Questions to Consider

1. In "Tango," the author uses this passionate dance as a metaphor for relationships. How is a relationship like a tango?
2. What other metaphors could be used to describe a relationship?

# White/Black

## Constance Campbell

2004


White are the clouds that striate the blue sky
Black is the night and the color of the eyes
White is what was wanted a long time ago,
Black is what I have grown fond to know.
Here is the story that goes way back
When I had a love for white never wanted black.
Growing up in the ghetto was all I knew
Truly I didn't want black eyes, instead I wanted blue
Dirty blond hair and a straight cute nose
Little lips to kiss and no Afros.
He was my white that's all I could take
I loved him each day cuz he looked like Justin Timberlake.
White was acting like the black man encompassed in white skin
Why was he what I wanted, I couldn't help but dig in
Dig into my conscience and out of the darkness that was blocking
my sight
Right out of my white love into the sea of the night.
The dark embraces that held me so close
Black came in different colors caramel, yellow, dark, brown, and
burnt toast
These things came as images surrounding my mind
Why didn't I notice black first cuz white was what I wanted to find.
As black became more intriguing, I slowly let go of white
Didn't want to let go, but I was being called by the night.
I still wanted to have the straight nose, blond hair, and blue eyes
But not as much as I wanted the six pack, built chest and arms, and
Ooo those muscular thighs.

You see white could not touch me, squeeze me, and grab me around my waist
With a grip that made me shiver and rid me from my taste
Now white had some things to offer but black had more to give
I don't know if I'll go back to white again because I would rather live
Live for the black in me and black bodies and their chests
Psychologically, emotionally, physically black man is my only request.

## Questions to Consider

1. "White/Black" introduces a writer who changes her mind about love midway through the piece. Why does she change her mind? Do you think it's a change for the better?
2. Has this kind of change or reversal ever happened to you?

# How to Love a Black Man

## Justina Trimmings

2013

The first thing you must understand,
There is no easy way to love a black man.

You have to figure him out and know what he's about,
And know that he is someone you can't live without.

Shower him with sweetness,
But never let him take your kindness for weakness.

Be appreciative of the little things he tries to do.
It's hard for him to give himself to you.

Let him know he can confide in you,
And in return he won't hide things from you.

Be his friend, not his foe.
When he makes mistakes don't say, "I told you so".

Be understanding, not commanding.
He's facing a world that is so demanding.
Don't get too cozy in your comfort zone.
You'll take him for granted and end up alone.

Keep loving exciting, do the best you can,
Because there is no easy way to love a black man.

## Questions to Consider

1. In "How to Love a Black Man," what advice is the author giving readers?
2. How would this piece be similar or different if it were simply titled "How to Love a Man"?
3. What advice, if any, could you give about how to love a black man?

# Mister Misunderstood: Dedicated to My Champ

## Ms. Terehas

2004


Behind his baby face and masculine frame,
Lies shadows of his past painted with struggles and pain,
A struggle with wanting to start doing what's right,
And the pain of coming back to this reality called life,
Mister Misunderstood been thuggin' and runnin' the streets,
But to me he reveals his other side that's deliciously sweet,

My thug nigga, always has a unit on his face so mean,
But makes sure that he's treating me like his Nubian queen,
Mister Misunderstood has a good head on his shoulders,
And I've grown to respect him as we age and get older,
He says that I used to try him, but I wish that he knew,
The only reason was because I knew what his charm could do.

Mister Misunderstood, is my champion,
Been trying eight years to be my only satisfaction,
Total knock out baby, I surrender my all,
I'm just scared that one day he won't be there to catch me when I fall,
Mister Misunderstood is not what they say,
In fact he's better than that, in each and every way,
I can't deny it, it caught me by surprise,
Little Luther, so grown up and wise,
Every time I look at you, you smile back at me,
Keeping me pinching myself hoping that it's not a dream,

I just wish everyone could see what I see,
Cause I'm holding it down 'til the day they set you free.
I never knew that it could feel this good,
I guess you really are Mister Misunderstood.

## Questions to Consider

1. Why does the author believe that the subject of this piece is being misunderstood?
2. Where was Mister Misunderstood while this piece is being written?
3. Do you think the writer's sense of injustice for her man has strengthened her love?

# A Man's Voice

## Joseph McLemore

**2006**

Believe it or not, some of us will cook you dinner and run your bath water.
On you, some of us will spend our last quarter.

There are some of us who aren't afraid to love or be in love.
Some of us prefer staying home, instead of going to the club.

Some of us enjoy being intimate with your mind, body and soul.
And then there are some of us that won't date you if you keep your legs closed.

Some of us don't have a problem telling you the truth.
Others of us lie in order to protect you.

Some of us aren't able to get you that Gucci purse, Marc Jacobs or Seven jeans.
For some of us Forever 21 and Payless are the only stores within our means.


Sometimes we confuse showing we care for being soft.
And some of our perceptions of a real man may be a little off.

Some of us may watch America's Top Model instead of the big game,
But ladies, for your broken hearts, us men aren't always to blame.

## Questions to Consider

1. "A Man's Voice" sheds some light on the man's point of view in a relationship. What is the man's perspective in this piece?
2. What is this man willing to do for his woman?
3. Have you ever met a man like this?

# You Are the First Man I Ever Loved

## Anonymous

2006

As a young girl I thought that you were the biggest, strongest, and sweetest man in the world, but by the time I was eleven, you and mom split, and I saw a different side of you. I saw the cheating, selfish, and thoughtless side of you. You left my sister and me in a household with a mother who was so deeply depressed from your betrayal, that she barely spoke to us unless it was to curse or beat us for simply looking like you. All the while you were enjoying your new life and new family in Miami. When you stopped paying child support, mom could no longer make ends meet so we were forced to move to Miami to live with Uncle Richard. The move to Miami put us in the same city as you and yet we barely spent time with you. It took divine intervention, in the form of what doctors called "your deathbed", to bring us back together. The road to restoring our damaged relationship has been very hard work but I must say that our relationship today is stronger than I ever could have imagined. This entire experience has taught me the art of forgiveness. So daddy, I guess that it is safe to say that you were the first man I have ever loved, the first man that I have ever hated, and the first man I have ever forgave and loved again.

## Questions to Consider

1. What are some of the many emotions the author of "You Are the First Man I Ever Loved" expresses about her father?
2. How do her emotions change over the course of her essay? Why do they change?
3. How does she feel about her father by the end of the piece? Do you think her feelings are justified?

# Thank You

## Alana Debose

2012

Thank you
For listening and not just hearing me,
For entertaining my outlandish dreams,
And for believing I could achieve those dreams too.

Thank you
For cooking for me when I'm too lazy,
For cleaning up before I can finish making a mess,
And for explaining how and why because the answers are
important to me.

Thank you
For allowing me to fall apart,
For seeing me through the roughest time in my life,
And for showing that you never lost hope that I'd recover.

Thank you
For giving me good and bad examples,
For admitting you could have done better,
And for proving not all men are worthless.

Ultimately, thank you for loving me, Daddy.

## Questions to Consider

1. How does the author of "Thank You" feel about her father? Why does she feel this way?
2. How does this father-daughter relationship compare with the one described in "You Are the First Man I Ever Loved"?

# My First Love

## Kevin D. Tate

2002

When I first met you, my life was chaotic.
I had no direction; I had no strength; I had no peace.
I was timid, not wanting to know you.
But I wanted you to know me.
I played games with you; not taking you seriously;
knowing that you were serious all along.

I was ashamed to introduce you to my family,
friends, loved ones or even casual acquaintances.
I did not trust you.
I wanted you to notice me but I was not noticing you.

As storms came into my life,
lies and broken promises began to overwhelm me.
I had no place to go; I had no place to turn.
And then that is when you told me to come back to you.

There was no way that I thought that you would accept
pieces of a broken man, but you did.
I was hesitant at first, even afraid.
But as I began to spend more time with you,
I began to see the love that you have always had for me.
Amazingly, as I told more and more people about you,
I saw that others do not love you the same way that I do
or maybe they just have a hard time showing you.
Oh, but only if I could tell them that your love is
truly the only love that matters.

Friends, associates, family, loved ones will come and go.
But you and only you, will not break promises,
stand me up or disappoint me.
Not only are you wonderful
But you are excellent in every sense of the word.

I cannot believe that it has been five years
Since I told you that I wanted you,
But it has, and I do not regret my decision one bit.
Now I know without a shadow of a doubt

That what we have going,
no one can come between us.

Through it all God, I Love You!

## Questions to Consider

1. In "My First Love," a young man is writing about a completely different kind of love. At what point did you figure out what he was actually writing about?
2. What clues did the writer give throughout the piece that this was a different kind of relationship?

# Reflections

1. In this chapter the authors speak about several different types of love. What types of love do they address? What other types of love do you think about?
2. Did any of these pieces surprise you? If so, how?
3. All but one of the pieces in this chapter are written in first person. Which one was not? Which perspective did this author use? Why do you think so many of the authors used the first person point of view to write about this topic?

# Journal Prompts

1. Make a web that consists of the names of the people you love most. Now write a personal essay detailing why you love each one of them.
2. Respond to the following prompt in two or three different ways. A relationships is like a … because …
3. Write a card, letter, or email (no texts!) to someone you love saying why you love him or her. Send it!
4. Do you think our feelings about people are the most passionate feelings we are capable of? Write a humorous poem about something you love, such as chocolate, kittens, football, etc., or something that you don't love, such as broccoli, early mornings, rude people, etc.
5. Write about your relationship with your parents separately or together. How do you feel about your mother? Your father?
6. Do you think our relationships with our parents have an impact on our future love relationships? If so, how? Write about an example from your own life.

# CHAPTER 5: FAITH

*The assurance of all things hoped for*

## How important is faith in your life? Do you have a personal relationship with a higher power?

As you will see from the pieces included in this section, these authors clearly do have such a relationship. Faith, religion, belief in a higher power, and the expression of a personal relationship with God was a recurring theme in many of these essays. Some of the selections praise the Lord, some ask earnest and honest questions, and others plead for help or intervention.

In "Ignite My Fire," the writer is searching for ways to serve and be of use to the Lord. She writes in God's voice, "I want you to come and labor for me ... so that people will know to worship me."

In "A Letter to My Creator," the author sincerely questions whether or not she is "enough," and on days when she feels she isn't, she thanks God for his reassurance that she is. "Every day I am concerned with my future and if I will be successful enough."

The piece titled "Who Is My God?" is a series of poems explaining the many roles God plays in the author's life. She describes God as a peacemaker, companion, healer, savior, and more.

The humorous piece "Amen, Amen" talks about going to church every Sunday to "catch some of dat holy gos!" The writer goes on to tell us that the "pastor sure can put on a show … talkin' about Shedrach, Meschah and Abidingo."

The author of "The Model Prayer" writes about wanting to pray the perfect prayer. In her hectic life, she often finds herself just saying a quick prayer rather than taking the time to pray "correctly." Her prose poem is her attempt at doing it right.

The final piece, "Helplessly Scared," speaks to what one does on receiving a desperate phone call in the middle of the night from a friend who lives clear across the country—a friend who is being abused and beaten by her boyfriend. How does this writer feel? What can she do?

Faith, religion, belief in a higher power, and the expression of a personal relationship with God are common themes in these diverse works. What they all have in common is the writers' conviction and complete trust in the existence of a higher power. Their faith provides them with assurance of all things hoped for.

# Ignite My Fire

## Angel L. Garner

2008

Ignite my fire, Lord
I want to burn for you.
I intercede for this nation,
So they will burn, too.

Lord I know that you are searching,
For willing vessels through and through.
So bad my heart desires,
To be with you.

Excited, joyful, and eager,
I thought about how this marriage would be.
You see this divine man, came and called me.
Angel, He said, I want you to come and labor for me.
Do something in this nation, so that people will know to worship me.

Give them the news without a fuss or a fight,
And let them know I am the way, the truth and the light.
And this walk with me is by faith and not by sight.
And, Angel tell them to get ready because I'm coming back like a
thief in the night.
I will be looking for one without a spot or wrinkle in sight.
One who lives each day for me, as if it's their last night.

My child, you hold a key to how many will take flight,
Or choose to do wrong over right.

So get on your game and make sure it's tight.
Because this job you are on, it must be done right.
So let my spirit lead you and you will be alright.
And daughter you know, your fire was ignited that same night,
That you declared I was the way, the truth and your light!

## Questions to Consider

1. The poem "Ignite My Fire" is like a call and response. Who is calling out, and about what?
2. Who is responding? What is the responder saying to the caller?
3. What is the "news" the responder wants the caller to share?

# A Letter to My Creator

## Ashley Curtis

2015

You know me better than anyone else does, even better than I know myself. You know my strengths and weaknesses, my fears and my confidences, my heart and my mind. You made me this way: kind-hearted, nice, loyal, giving and loving. But then there's the other side of me mean, angry, spiteful and sometimes bitter. I'm sure you made me with all intentions of helping know when to use which side of me. I'm happy with who I am (most of the time), but I do have some concerns.

What if who I am is not good enough?

Should I change who YOU have created me to be, just to be liked?

Should I be working toward building a better me? Why? Aren't I supposed to be this woman? If not, then I wouldn't be right? You said that you made me in your image and in your likeness (Genesis 5:1-2) so why do I have to change who I am?

Why do I feel the need to change my personality, my characteristics, my way of life just to be accepted by a world who doesn't even know who they are? Now I see why in your word you said "Be in the world but not of the world." (John 2:15-17).

Every day I am concerned with my future and if I will be successful enough. I wonder if I will ever be in a good space, in life where there are no worries. Now I'm beginning to understand that, that's not how life works. I don't believe you want your creation to become satisfied and complacent in life. Sometimes I think you cause things to happen so that I don't become complacent with where I am in life. You want me to push for more. You want me to have the very best. That's why you cause some heartaches, that's why I lose friends, that's why sometimes I feel like I lose "everything." You're pushing me further. You are taking me out of my comfort zone.

I wish that sometimes you could come down out of the clouds and place your hand on my heart and allow it all to disappear. Sometimes I wonder why you can't do that, but then I remember that my faith must make me whole.

I know sometimes I forget to pray and I'm moving so fast that I forget to enjoy the moments in life but I want you to know that I am more than grateful, thankful, and appreciative of the many miracles you give me daily. I'll never forget how far I've come in life. I've always put myself in bad situations and you didn't allow me to be trapped by them. I'm sure there were a lot of accidents, conversations, diseases, pregnancies, and bad opportunities from which you have saved me.

Thank you for being reassuring on days where I don't feel too good about myself. Thank you in advance for the turn around that will take place. I know that the woman I will become will be great and I'm looking forward to meeting her.

I LOVE YOU

Your creation,

Ashley

## Questions to Consider

1. What dilemma is the writer facing and expressing in "A Letter to My Creator"?
2. In this piece, the writer quotes scripture. Where in the letter does she do this? What does she say through her use of scripture?

# Who Is My God?

Lois Harmon

2011

God
I Am
Alpha and Omega
Of precious eternal essence
Lord

Just
Jehovah Tsidkenu
The Righteous One
Narrow Path of Integrity
Perfect

Sanctifier
Jehovah M'kaddesh
Holy, Holy, Holy,
The one who sets apart
Purifier

Emmanuel
Jehovah Shammah
Never leaves me
One who is omnipresent
Companion

Supplier
Jehovah Jireh
Supplies my needs
Full of lasting wealth
Giver

Victorious
Jehovah Nissi
Reigns in Victory
One who is omnipotent
Warrior

Peacemaker
Jehovah Shiloh
Prince of Peace
Makes peace with enemies
Mediator

Healer
Jehovah Rapha
Stripes of healing
Heals sickness and disease
Restorer

Jesus
He saves
Delivers from sin
Giver of eternal life
Savior
God
The Father
Saves sinners instantly
Spirit of true holiness
Trinity

## Questions to Consider

1. "Who Is My God?" is a series of unrhymed diamante poems placed together to convey a cohesive message. In looking at each stanza, how would you describe this type of poem? Do you see any patterns within the verses?
2. This author uses many names to describe her God. What are some of those names? What are some other names for God?

# Amen, Amen

## Karwynn D. Paul

1994

Da church was all crowded, da ushers
was at day post, everybody had showed up,
to catch some of dat holy gos. Da deacons
was in day corner, the muthas was on da
other side, "amen, amen" towards da precha
dats what one deacon cried.

Da choir got up and sang my song, and
Got dat church a rollin, while precha was
in da pulpit, talking bout who had lied,
cheated and stolen. Den he really got
cranked up, cause pastor can put on a
show, he started talking bout Sheddrach,
Meschach, and Abindigo.

At da end of his surmon, peoples
was all at day feet; day had hurd
enufff of the word; to las dem thru
da week.

## Questions to Consider

1. "Amen, Amen" has a very distinctive voice. You can almost
   hear the writer speaking the words. Why do you think the
   author chose this voice?
2. What does this voice tell you about the person who is
   "speaking" in the poem?

# The Model Prayer

## Krystal Sheppard

**2008**

Dear God,

I love you and I praise your name.
With all that I have and all that I am I magnify you.
Lord you are worthy to be praised.
From the rising of the sun, to the going down of the same, I praise you.
Through the good and the bad, I praise you.
When all of my money is gone, I still praise you.
When I'm weary, head bowed, and heavy leaden, I'll praise you.
Lord, your word says "whatever is bound on earth shall be bound in heaven and
whatever is loosed on earth shall be loosed in heaven".
Lord, I loose joy, peace, and all the fruits of the spirit.
I bind everything that is set against me.
Lord, your work is a lamp unto my feet and a light unto my path,
so give me the desire to follow you.
Help me seek your face and live in your presence.
Lord, you are Jehovah Jireh, my provider.
You give me everything I need.
Lord you are Jehovah Rapha, my healer.
By your stripes I've been set free.
Lord God, your word says "seek ye first the Kingdom of God and His righteousness and
all these things will be added unto me".
Proverbs 31 says; "For who can find a virtuous woman? For her price is far above
rubies". Favor is deceitful, and beauty is vain, but a woman that reverences the Lord
shall be praised.

Help me to be a virtuous woman that reverences you.

Lord, like Moses, Abraham, Joshua, Isaac, Jacob, and all the great and mighty leaders,

help me to slay giants.

Help me to knock down the walls of Jericho

Open parted waters and help me to walk through them when all odds are set against me.

Help me to lead people into the Promised Land.

Lord, I want to be used by you.

You are the Potter and I am the clay...Mold me.

Lord, your eyes are in every place beholding the evil and the good...Control me.

You said, your work will not return unto you void, but will accomplish everything that it

is sent to accomplish......Guide me.

## Questions to Consider

1. In this prose/narrative poem, God is seen to be many things. What are some of the different roles God plays in this writer's life?
2. Are there other roles that you think are often ascribed to God?
3. Are any of these other roles applicable to this writer's situation?

# Helplessly Scared

## Jenay Gurdon

2015


Sitting here,
Feeling so helpless.
Not knowing what to do.
Not knowing how I can help.
Just praying
Because praying is the only thing I know I can do.
What do you do when your friend calls crying in the middle of the night and
You are a thousand miles away?
Not knowing what's wrong, because all you hear are her sobs.
When she finally talks, she tells you she is scared,
Scared of the man she loves,
Scared of his threats,
And whether he will fulfill them.
As you listen to her you feel her pain,
Feel her terror!
Then he comes,
You hear her scream,
Hear the two going back and forth.
Then all of a sudden, there is a silence.
You scream her name over and over!
There is no answer.


Then he comes to the phone
Telling you how your friend is crazy,
He gives her the phone and she is huffing and puffing,
Short of breath.

The man she loves has just choked her and drug her outside.
The phone disconnects.
I am at a loss as to what to do.
So I do the only thing I know?
I bend my knees and pray.

## Questions to Consider

1. What is the author praying for in this poem? Do you think she is asking for consolation, advice, or intervention?
2. Other than praying, what else do you think she could or should have done in the situation described? What might have prevented her from doing this?

# Reflections

1. Two of the poems included in this section on faith are written almost like conversations. Which two? How are the conversations in the two poems similar? How are they different?

2. Two of the works in this section are written as letters to God. Which two? Why do you think the authors chose this form to express their feelings and ask their questions? One letter is answered in the poem, while the other is not. Why do you think this second letter goes unanswered? Do you think the lack of answer indicates that the author's letter wasn't received? Explain why or why not?

3. Although all of these writings invoke their writers' relationships with God, only one actually describes a church-related experience. What does this say about the difference between religion and faith?

4. Make a list of <u>ten</u> different emotions. How many of these did you find in these selections? Did this surprise you? Why or why not? Use specific examples from the poems to support the emotions you identified.

5. Which of the works in this section did you find most meaningful? Why/how did it touch you?

# Journal Prompts

1. Write your own letter to God or a higher power. What will you say in this letter? What will you ask for?

2. Most everyone has been to a church or other place of worship. What was your impression of this place? What did you see, hear, smell, etc.? Write a sensory poem about this experience.

3. How important is faith in your life? Write about your own personal relationship with a higher power. If you do not have one, write about why you do not.
4. Using the poem "Who is My God?" as a model, write a poem in the diamante style about any topic of your own choice.

# CHAPTER 6: HOPE

*A strong and confident expectation for a positive outcome related to the future*

## What is your greatest hope? What do you hope for the future?

Most of the authors of the pieces in this chapter were juniors and seniors at a university where they were training to become elementary school teachers. Perhaps by virtue of their chosen profession, their youthfulness, or even their own nearness to graduation, the future (especially as it concerned children) was often a theme in their writing.

This chapter includes "Come Up, Black Man," in which the author beseeches black fathers to "take hold of your plight, hold up your families, and do what's right." He expresses a confident expectation for the future of these fathers and their children.

In "Peace and Harmony" the author expresses her hope for a peaceful and harmonious world. She longs for a place where "there will be no more hatred or crime, just peace and harmony all the time."

"A Letter to My Unborn Child" reveals a woman contemplating her as yet unconceived children. She tells them, "I am in college, preparing myself ... trying to be the best I can be for you." Perhaps her hope is also their hope?

Written in 2008, "Yes, We Can!" expresses the author's "hope for a change, hope in a man, President Barack Obama … . Yes, we can!" America's first black president had been elected, and for many, hope was finally in the air.

In the piece titled "The Age of Innocence," the author expresses "so many high hopes for better moments" to come. She addresses her hope for the children of the future.

The last piece, "The Classroom Gardener," was written by the author of this book as a final message to her students, all future teachers. "I plant seeds of knowledge and bits of wisdom, too."

All of these selections are looking forward and expressing a sense of hopefulness for a better future. All these young writers were sharing their belief that better things are possible for all.

# Come Up, Black Man

## Eric Benjamin

2006

Black man there is a cry in the hearts of your children today.
Come up and meet them and show them the way

The aches and pains are too much for a child to bear.
Even if you don't act like you care.

God is watching with his all seeing eye,
As the world looks on with hate and despise.

Come up Black Man, take hold of your given plight,
Hold up your families and do what's right.

A yearning heart for a dad to be near,
Could lead to destruction, pain and fear.

It's time to show the children, they are not alone,
Now its time for you to take care of your own.

## Questions to Consider

1. In this piece, what does the author want black men to do? Why does he want them to do this?
2. What do you think his purpose was in writing this?

# Peace and Harmony

## Linelle Young

1993

Take me to a beautiful place,
Where I've never been before.
Where hope is written on everyone's face,
And we all know what's in store.

There will be no more hatred or crime,
No more backbiting or self-destruction,
Just peace and harmony all the time,
With no kind of ugly obstruction.

Hope and love, these are the keys
To unlock any door.
To a place where we won't have to see,
The cruelty anymore.

So come on women, men, boys and girls,
Let's join hands and sing.
A peaceful harmony throughout the world,
Where hope will reign supreme.

## Questions to Consider

1. In "Peace and Harmony," what does the author hope for in the future?
2. What are your hopes for the future of our world?

# To My Unborn Child

## Lanijah Greer

2014

To my unborn child, I love you more than life itself. There will never be enough days in a year for me to express how deeply I feel about you. You are my biggest blessing in life. I thank God for you every spare second that I get. I don't care if you have ten toes or no toes at all, or if you have fair skin or dark skin. I will tell you every day that you are the most beautiful thing in the entire world.

To my unborn child, if you are a boy, I apologize in advance for the stereotypes you have been born into. It will never be your fault if people judge you based upon the color of your skin. I want you to always keep your head up and never bow down to anyone. Always know that mommy is your biggest fan. Whatever you choose to be in life, I will always be in your corner encouraging you, loving you, and supporting you every step of the way. Don't let negative peer pressure get to you. ALWAYS REMEMBER THAT, if you feel like you are spiraling out of control, come to me. I will never steer you wrong. Son, always remember to treat your women the way you would treat your mom; nothing but love and respect. At all times. No matter the situation.

To my unborn child, if you are a girl, I promise to not only be your mother but your best friend. I will always remember my experiences when I was your age so I will understand your issues like not being "pretty enough" or "good enough" or "smart enough", but I promise to tell you ever day that you are enough. If anyone tells you otherwise, they are not deserving of you. To my unborn daughter, always remember your worth. You are a beautiful queen. And on the days that you feel like a peasant, come to me and I'll remind you of your royalty. Daughter, I want you to go to school and become whatever you desire because I will support you nevertheless.

To my unborn child, I am preparing myself for you. I am in school trying to be the best that I can be for you. I promise not to bring you into this world until I have reached my full potential. I love you more than I love myself. And whenever you feel anything other than love and happiness, refer back to this letter to reassure you that you are God's greatest creation.

## Questions to Consider

1. In "To My Unborn Child," the writer is looking forward to her future family. If you could, what would you tell your as yet unborn or unconceived children about how you are preparing yourself for them?
2. Do you think the author of this piece will be a good mother? Why or why not?
3. Do you think you will be a good mother/father? Why or why not?

# Yes, We Can!

## Keri Ousley

**2008**

Roaring, cheering, It's all so loud.
In the presence of my own home screaming,
"I'm black and I'm proud!"

Blacks, Whites, Mexicans,
All in unison,
YES WE CAN!!!

It's been a long journey,
It's been so tough,
This time we showed them
We've all just had enough

"It's time for a change!"
He caught our attention,
We were all in awe with everything he said.
Everything he mentioned.

He's so real,
He's so sincere,
Some of the things he said
Made me shed a tear.

Barack Obama,
Our 44th president,
There was no cheating this time
The fair win was evident.

Some may talk,
Some may hate,
Some may make inappropriate remarks.
But this time it was fate.

This victory is for our ancestors.
The ones who fought hard,
The ones who fought long,
The ones who risked their lives
So we could sing a happier song.

Rosa Parks,
Martin Luther King,
Are just a few of the many
That let their voices ring.

They helped pave the way,
They helped shine the light,
So that our future would be more
Clear, and Oh so bright.

So now we finally made it,
We're finally here.
A new dawn, a new day,
A new future is near.
Hope for a change,
Hope in a man,
President Barack Obama…
YES WE CAN!!!

## Questions to Consider

1. "Yes, We Can!" is not about the hope of an individual but rather the hope of a people, the hope of a nation. Do you think this hope has been realized? Why or why not?

# Age of Innocence
## Callie Hill
**2015**

Children and their love
Children and their trust
Children and their teachers

Eager eyes and welcoming arms
Words are pouring for me to hear
Dirty hands and messy clothes
Yearning to play at the playground

The classroom of learning
Kids in their seats listening
Their supplies are beside them
Eyes are scrambling to focus
They are trying to resist their classroom friend

Hands go in the air
The kids all want to share
Key phrases are learned
Their behavior is managed
Nowhere else can you find a place like this
Such unique and open individuals
So much to share, to learn, and to still remain accepting
The kids all want approval
They all want attention
There is no judgement here

Real honesty pours with no hatred
Only fleeting moments of sadness
So many high hopes for better moments
Children and their love
Children and their trust
Children and their teachers

## Questions to Consider

1. What is the author's message in this piece?
2. What are this author's hopes for the future?
3. What are *your* hopes for the children of the future?

# The Classroom Gardener

## Gail Bauman

2008

I plant seeds of knowledge
and bits of wisdom, too.
I nurture with experience
and information, too.

I pat the soil with kindness
and model what to do.
I watch for signs of growth
to come pushing through.

I sprinkle my seedlings with encouragement
and teach them how to think.
I show them that from storms
they must never shrink.

I place my seedlings in the sun,
so they can feel its light.
I feed them with motivation,
so they can do what's right.

I wait patiently for signs of growth
to mature and sprout.
I tend my seedlings in the classroom
waiting for leaves of insight to come out.

I watch the plants and then the flowers
as they come into their own.

I reflect upon my garden
and the seeds I've sown.

I watch them blossom and mature,
drop new seeds and then,
I watch these seeds take root in a child's mind,
to start the cycle once again.

## Questions to Consider

1. In this final piece, "The Classroom Gardener," what is the author's message to her students?
2. What is her hope for the future?
3. Why do you think this piece was chosen to be the final selection in this book?

# Reflections

1. From where do you think these young people draw their hope?
2. Do you think there is a relationship between hope for oneself and hope in general?
3. In looking at all the selections in this chapter, which one do you think represents a hope that can easily be realized? Which represents a hope that is, perhaps, unattainable?
4. Hope is expressed in different ways by these authors. For some it seems to be wishful thinking, while for others it is a call to action. How would you characterize the hope expressed in each selection?

# Journal Prompts

1. Write a letter to your future children or grandchildren. Tell them what you are doing to prepare to be your best for them.
2. Write a letter to the children of the future. What are you doing to prepare the world for them?
3. What are your hopes for the future of the world in general? Make a web of at least ten things you hope for the future. Now, write about these hopes and what you can do to help realize them.
4. An earlier chapter featured writings about faith. How is faith the same as and/or different from hope? Draw a diagram comparing and contrasting faith and hope. Write about their similarities and differences.

# THE POWER OF WRITING: SOME FINAL THOUGHTS

As you have seen from reading the words of these young authors, they care deeply about the world in which they live. They think deeply and analyze their circumstances and surroundings. They write and express themselves from their own unique perspectives as young people of color.

Through their writing, these authors reveal a full spectrum of human emotion—heartfelt sadness, joy, grief, despair, happiness, love, and more. For many of these authors, writing was a powerful tool that often unleashed unexpected feelings and thoughts. One of the authors of a particularly difficult and emotional piece commented that writing about that painful incident helped her to ease the pain she had always carried with her. In this way, writing can be cathartic and therapeutic.

Writing can also capture moments in time. It can preserve the thoughts and feelings we had at a certain juncture in our lives. As one of the authors noted about her writing many years later, it was like opening a time capsule. Another author offered tears of joy after rereading her piece for the first time in twenty years. It was like reconnecting with an old friend.

Writing together helped break down boundaries. Writing together helped us to know each other better. Writing together bound us together. Writing together is what has kept us connected.

These writers have gone on to become playwrights, bankers, business people, school district administrators, consultants, counselors, vice presidents, assistant principals and principals, but most importantly, teachers—classroom teachers from Fort Lauderdale to Atlanta, from California to New York and from Detroit to Dubai. Teachers. Hopefully, teachers who teach writing.

Writing has the power to inspire, to motivate, to entertain, to provoke thought, to inform, to enlighten, and so much more. We hope that these *Voices of Color* have inspired, motivated, entertained, provoked, informed, and enlightened you!

www.ingramcontent.com/pod-product-compliance
Lightning Source LLC
Chambersburg PA
CBHW050524280326
41932CB00014B/2452